The Picnic

Written by Stephen Cosgrove

Illustrated by Ilona Steelhammer

IDEALS CHILDREN'S BOOKS

Copyright © MCMLXXXVIII by DreamMaker, Inc.
All rights reserved.
Printed and bound in the United States of America.
Published by Ideals Publishing Corporation,
Nelson Place at Elm Hill Pike,
Nashville, Tennessee 37214

ISBN 0-8249-8278-9

Dedicated to my dear friend Robert Crosby.
He has spent his life in the town of Simplicity
in the Land of Candor and is a Simple Folk indeed.
Stephen

Once there was a tiny house built upon a single hill and nestled all alone in the forest in the Land of Candor.

Here a lady lived all alone, and she was called the Lady Lonely.
She had a garden that she weeded and

seeded. She had a barn that she built with boards. But she lived all alone and had no friends.

What she had, instead, were two bunnies, a
goose, and a duck named Fred.

They loved the Lady Lonely because she was
what she was and they liked the food she fed.

But the Lady Lonely was very lonely living all alone in the country.

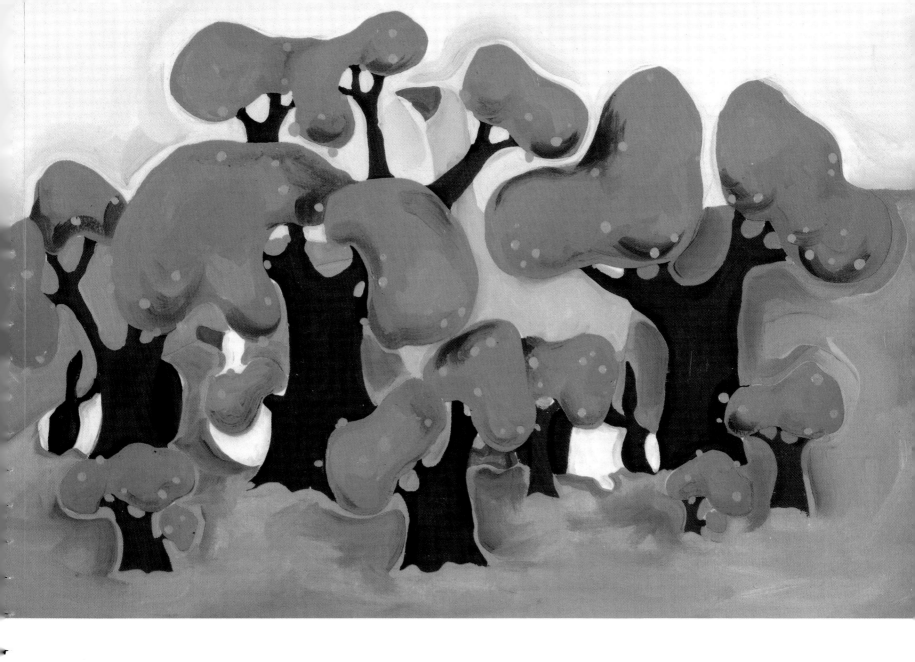

One day she looked about her farm. She looked and looked, but all that she could see was open space that was oh, so empty.

That very day she decided to pack all her things in a wooden wheelbarrow. And she was off to find friends on the path straight and narrow.

When all was packed, down the path she fled with two bunnies, a goose, and a duck named Fred.

She could see in the distance a little town busily bustling. Fred was so excited, his feathers kept rustling.

The goose and the bunnies were feeling kind
of friskety. For they knew they would find friends
in the town called Simplicity.

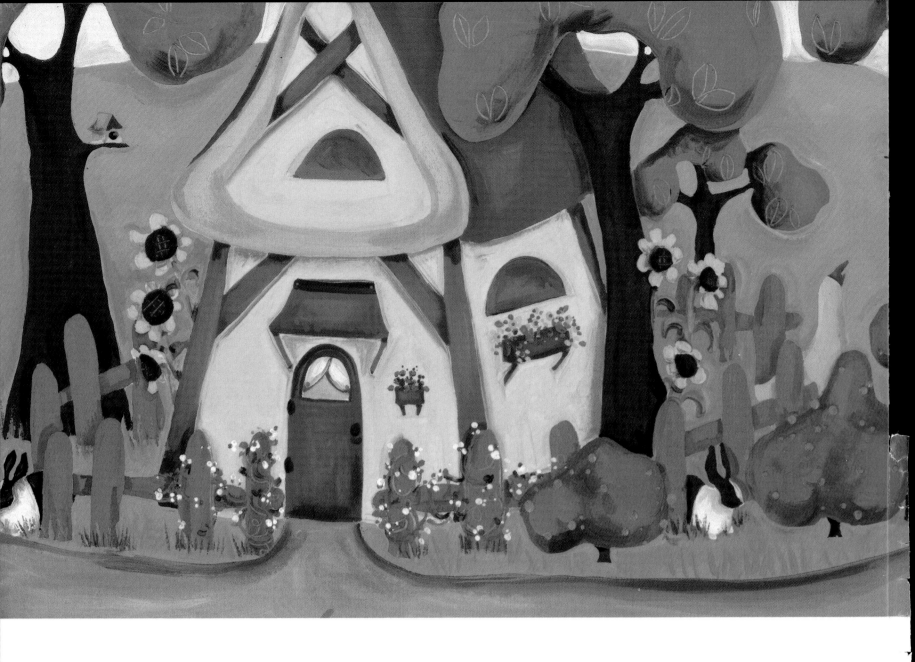

They walked and walked until they reached
the town.

There they bought a cottage with flowers all around.

Lady Lonely unpacked and hung a picture,
it was said, surrounded by her pets: two bunnies, a goose, and a duck named Fred.

She sat on her porch and watched the simple folk walk by. Of course, she didn't say hello or goodbye for Lady Lonely was a bit shy.

"I know," she said, "I'll pack a picnic . . . a picnic lunch. Then all the folk will come to munch."

She rustled and bustled, cooking this and that. And when she was through she put on her hat.

To the park she went with her hat on her head, followed by two bunnies, a goose, and a duck named Fred.

She spread her food but nobody came. She
waited and waited. Tsk, tsk, what a shame.

But the Lady Lonely wasn't really alone anymore or even before. For she had always been surrounded by friends, it was said . . .

two bunnies, a goose, and a duck named
Fred.

For that's what the simple folk do . . .